Title Information:	
Date:	
Logbook #:	
Continued from Logbook#	
Name:	
Title:	
Address:	
City & State:	
Email address:	
Telephone #:	
Date Logbook Started:	
Date Logbook Ended:	
Signature	
Notes:-	

MW01242496

TABLE OF CONTENTS		
DATE	SUBJECTS	PAGE #

TABLE OF CONTENTS

DATE	SUBJECTS	PAGE #

TABLE OF CONTENTS

DATE	SUBJECTS	PAGE #

TABLE OF CONTENTS		
DATE	SUBJECTS	PAGE #

	Date	Page #: 1
	___/___/___	Book #:

	Date	Page #: 5
	___/___/___	Book #:

	Date	Page #: 17
	___/___/___	Book #:

	Date	Page #: 19
_____	___/___/___	Book #:

	Date	Page #: 21
	___/___/___	Book #:

	Date	
	___/___/___	Book #:

	Date ___/___/___	Page #: 23
		Book #:

	Date	
	___/___/___	Book #:

	Date ___/___/___	Page #: 29
		Book #:

	Date ___/___/___	Page #: 35
		Book #:

	Date	Page #: 37
————————————	___/___/___	Book #:

	Date	Page #: 38
	___/___/___	Book #:

	Date ___/___/___	Page #: 41
		Book #:

	Date	Page #: 43
	___/___/___	Book #:

	Date ___/___/___	Page #: 45
		Book #:

	Date	Page #: 46
	___/___/___	Book #:

	Date ___/___/___	Page #: 47
		Book #:

	Date	Page #: 48
	___/___/___	Book #:

	Date	Page #: 52
	___/___/___	Book #:

	Date ___/___/___	Page #: 56
		Book #:

	Date	Page #: 60
_____	___/___/___	Book #:

	Date	Page #: 65
	___/___/___	Book #:

	Date	Page #: 71
	___/___/___	Book #:

	Date	Page #: 75
_____	___/___/___	Book #:

	Date	Page #: 77
	___/___/___	Book #:

	Date	
	___/___/___	Book #:

	Date	Page #: 82
_____	___/___/___	Book #:

	Date	
	___/___/___	Book #:

	Date ___/___/___	Page #: 94
		Book #:

	Date ___/___/___	Page #: 95
		Book #:

Made in the USA
Middletown, DE
18 September 2023